Scarred Resilience

Scarred Resilience

Poems by

Suzanne Cottrell

© 2021 Suzanne Cottrell. All rights reserved.
This material may not be reproduced in any form, published,
reprinted, recorded, performed, broadcast,
rewritten or redistributed without
the explicit permission of Suzanne Cottrell.
All such actions are strictly prohibited by law.

Cover design by Shay Culligan
Cover photograph by Sara Cottrell

ISBN: 978-1-954353-81-7

Kelsay Books
502 South 1040 East, A-119
American Fork, Utah, 84003

For my family, whose unconditional love and support see me through life's challenges.

Acknowledgments

Thanks to my family for their encouragement and support. Special thanks to my loving husband Bob and daughter Sara for their ideas, photographs, editing, and encouragement.

My appreciation goes to the Granville County Senior Center Writers' Group for critiquing my poems and inspiring me to keep writing.

Thanks to Anne Anthony, who encouraged me to submit my first micro fiction piece, "Sole Mate," and to Nicole Monaghan, Editor of *Nailpolish Stories, A Tiny and Colorful Literary Journal,* who accepted it and nineteen other pieces.

My thanks to the following journals, anthologies, and their editors:

Angel Poetry Magazine: "Yet, We Laughed"
Avocet, Journal of Nature Poems: "Essence Renewed"
Burningword Literary Journal: "Aged"
Cagibi Literary: "Wintry Liberation"
Gifts of the Seasons, Autumn and Winter (Kelsay Books, 2020): "Spiritual Awakening," "Wintry Liberation"
Gifts of the Seasons, Spring and Summer (Kelsay Books, 2021): "Bone Dry," "Essence Renewed," "Nature's Solace," "Remembrance," "River Gifts," "Solitary Walk"
Literary Yard: "Danger Below," "Worm-Ridden Republic"
Nailpolish Stories, a Tiny and Colorful Literary Journal: "Sole Mate"
Poetry Leaves: "Ascension"
Poetry Quarterly: "Remembrance," "Silent Stroll," "Spiritual Awakening," Winner of the 2017 Rebecca Lard Poetry Award (Prolific Press)
Proverse Hong Kong Poetry Prize, Mingled Voices #5: "Cast Iron Mother"

Scarlet Leaf Review: "Provider," "Resilient Reflection," "Survivor," "Web of Lies"
Tanka Journal: "Forsaken lovers," "Grandmother's treasure," "Penned Dear John letter," "Swinging their clasped hands"
The Dragon Poet Review: "Nature's Solace"
The Pangolin Review: "Adrift," "Merciless Storm," "No More Regrets"
The Remembered Arts Journal: "Bone Dry"
The Weekly Avocet: "River Gifts," "Solitary Walk"
Three Line Poetry: "Winding road lined with memories"
Twist in Time Literary Magazine: "Waning Time"
Women Speak: Portraits, Poetry, and Prose of the Feminine Experience by Nancy Smith, et.al.: "Altered Silhouette"

Contents

Spiritual Awakening	13
Wintry Liberation	14
Ice Storm	15
Sea Holly Lighthouse	16
Web of Lies	17
No More Regrets	18
Resilient Reflection	19
Onslaught Overcome	20
Ascension	21
Raven's Tale	22
Nature's Solace	23
Bone Dry	24
Survivor	25
Merciless Storm	26
Adrift	28
Short Poems	29
Sole Mate	30
Unacknowledged Truth	31
Cast Iron Mother	33
Altered Silhouette	34
Yet, We Laughed	35
Danger Below	36
Enlightened Silence	37
Harmonious Healer	38
Discarded	39
Transformation	41
Silent Stroll	42
Essence Renewed	43
Solitary Walk	44
Remembrance	45
Worm-Ridden Republic	46
River Gifts	47

Aged	49
Scarred Resilience	50
Virgo's Light	51
Waning Time	52

Spiritual Awakening

Hoarfrost glazes jade grass blades.
White yard glistens this December morning.
Dense, smoky fog settles as clouds hug the ground.
Brisk breeze kisses rosy cheeks.
A white orb, peeks through at the horizon.
Sun renders an eerie illumination.

Soul detaches from physical body,
Hang glides effortlessly above the cloaked terrain.
A river of emotions flood heightened consciousness.
Visual lenses adjust to the changing light.
Vivid images reveal miniscule surface details.

Like a rock climber resting on a narrow ledge
Examines panoramic view of life,
Places events in perspective.
Soft whisper instills, "It's not your time."
Fear of future no longer consumes.

Magnifying white light releases its gravitational pull.
Peace and love envelop spiritual essence.
Mind grapples with soul's re-entry into aging body,
Hesitating to forgo the transcendental experience.

As the fog lifts, sunlight transitions to golden mustard.
Frozen dew melts, creates water droplet prisms.
Winding asphalt absorbs wave lengths of light, radiates warmth,
Guides feet along earthly path.
Life's purpose redefined.

Wintry Liberation

Sheltered from
Blustery winds
Whiteout conditions
Siberian wind chill

Enveloped by a
Crackling fire's warmth
Settled comfortably
Eyes closed
Breathing naturally

In pursuit of
Mindful fitness
Freezing emotions to
Preserve cherished memories
Fluttering within a snow globe

Encouraging worldly thoughts
To lie dormant or
Drift through
Emptying any trash
Cleansing and liberating as the frigid air

Ice Storm

Temperatures plummeted,
frigid as an arctic night.
Wind howled, trunks shivered.

Freezing rain coated branches and wires.
Lights flickered, forewarned of power outage.
Icy stalactites dangled precariously.

Trees bore weight as long as they could.
Crackles, snaps, ice shards littered the ground.
House interior matched onyx sky.

We read books by flashlight
till snuggling under woolen
blankets lured us to bed.

Sea Holly Lighthouse

Sea holly stands on sandy dunes and shoreline.
Clusters of thistle-like steel blue blooms
wear crowns of silvery-green spiky leaves,
weather the storms and extreme temperatures.
Stalks, secured by deep tap roots, bend in coastal winds,
tolerate salty sea spray, resist drought.

Life's storms, unfulfilled desires,
feed my melancholy soul.
Tears, enough to fill an ocean,
I remain adrift searching for answers.

Where is a beacon to guide me?
Self-reliant sea holly lights the path.
Time to plant my roots,
stand firm but be flexible.

An unforeseen lighthouse

Web of Lies

It started with one tiny, white lie,
One sticky thread—
    already have plans.
Each lie escalated,
complicated relationships—
    feel sick,
     no money,
      love someone else.

No harm meant,
personal desires preempted
others' needs and wants.
Received fewer invitations,
friendships questioned.

Lips trembled, muscles tensed,
beads of sweat streaked down
pallid face, flinched as
web strands vibrated,
yielded struggling prey.

Alarm sounded, voice shrieked.
Time to think beyond oneself.
Cut the sticky fibers
before lies devour you.

No More Regrets

Abyss grows deeper, darker, colder.
Shrouds obscure souls from light and warmth.
Regrets accumulate, piles of discarded bones.
Worldly influences create universal suffering.
Life's circumstances and choices determine regrets.
If only, I had…

Retreat from the shadows of excuses,
Escape the caverns of denial,
Cast off the veil of disillusionment,
Climb the jagged walls,
Reach for opportunities,
Transform through new experiences.

Live and learn from past mistakes.
Time on earth runs short,
Judgment day nears,
Forgive yourself and others,
Change your heart, your life,
Live with no more regrets.

Resilient Reflection

I do not live in a perfect world,
so why am I upset
when I am not perfect?

Do I feel I have let
myself or others down?

Change in outward appearance
does not taint one's beauty within.

Bruised peaches can still be eaten.
Tattered pages can still be read.
Dirty clothes can still be worn.
Bumpy roads can still be traveled.

I must learn to
be confident,
acknowledge my mistakes,
platforms for growth,

be content with
my best efforts,
regardless of
the outcomes.

To be alive
is imperfection.

Onslaught Overcome

Day after day,
solar rays burn,
wind gusts chafe,
dust clouds choke,
sand grains scratch,
glass shards pierce.

Debris whirls as
jeering words ambush,
filth defiles,
fear envelopes,
hurt destroys,
self-esteem erodes.

Head bows,
shoulders hunch,
hands clutch,
feet shuffle,
seek refuge,
shield from barrage.

As frustration and
anger mount,
survival instinct
garners inner strength.
Stand erect,
hold head high.

Minimize interactions,
demonstrate impassivity,
restore confidence.

Storm dissipates.

Ascension

Rainbow hot air balloon ascends,
skirts outreaching branches,
avoids entanglement in spiteful words,

catches rising thermals,
uplifts my spirit,
dodges oppressive clouds.

Radiant sunbeams warm my being.
Inspiring vistas energize me.
Birds chirp encouragement.

Balloon cruises above negativity.
I enjoy the reassuring ride.
Grateful for prevailing
winds of optimism.

Like air,
I rise.

Raven's Tale

Within the recesses of my mind,
I hide among dark secrets and
conflicts, fearful of exposing the past.

A winged harbinger tries to
lure me out of the shadows
and into the light, caws a message.

My conscience mind
is unwilling to receive.
I struggle to accept the
truth of what I have become.

Yet, I must be courageous
and seek out answers, for how
can I heal if I'm not willing
to soar over obstacles?

Within my Zen garden,
four rocks carefully stacked
symbolize the need for balance
among my physical, emotional,
mental, and spiritual realms.

The perched raven
observes and waits.
Transformation requires
self-reflection
if only I were ready.

Nature's Solace

I sit on a slab of sun-warmed, red sandstone.
The breeze brushes back my hair,
massages my temples
as I strive to clear my mind.

Submerged legs in cool water,
resting weary feet on the stream bed,
sandy clay oozes between my toes.
Rushing water washes away worries.

I contemplate my distorted reflection.
Meditation swirls like water in an eddy.
Warbler's aria draws me to the present.
Breathe deeply, deliberately.

Lavender's scent helps me relax.
I attempt to liberate body, mind.
Nature's therapy—
In need of more sessions.

Bone Dry

Scorched, barren land
Blasts of arid wind
Blood orange dust swirled

Sizzling worn, pitted sandstone
Withered desert marigolds
Moisture depleted

Sunbaked skin
Parched lips
Unable to utter a word

Scent of dampness
Somber thundcrhcad
Momentarily hid the sun

Sank to her knees
Cocked back her head
Squeezed closed her eyes

Tongue extended
Yearned for a taste
Dirty tracks etched her face

Fleeting deluge
One cloud breathed life
Into her desert

Survivor

Smoldering air presses on my shoulders
Smoke lingers, lungs labor
Eyes water, I stumble among

Charred remains of broadleaf forest
Snap, crack, vibrations radiate up my legs
I lament over fallen trees, injured

Soldiers strewn like pick up
Sticks on a forgotten battlefield
Wounds ooze sap, limbs abscess

Causalities cry out, I cringe
Bone saw grates, chain saw roars
Surgeon removes a limb in hope

Of saving a sentinel,
I pray for nurturing rains,
Reseeding, and regrowth

Months pass before next visit
My eyes and smile widen as
I spot a chartreuse shoot near a

Slippery Elm's burly scar
Regrowth brings new life

Merciless Storm

Emergency sirens blared, too late to evacuate.
They sought shelter in first floor bathroom,
threw blankets and pillows over their bodies,
anticipated the hurricane's arrival.
They clutched each other, mumbled prayers.

Rain pelted roof with deafening drum beats,
surf surged and devoured the beach,
wind roared like a hungry beast.
Shingles surrendered and flew away.
Windows succumbed to pressure and exploded.
Battered walls buckled, wailed like victims under siege.

Boards splintered,
concrete cracked and crumbled.
They ducked their heads, closed their eyes,
pressed their hands over their ears.
Their bodies trembled.
They clutched each other, mumbled prayers.

Waited an eternity for the light of day,
finally they emerged to painful discoveries—
houses dismantled, property ruined,
buildings lifted off foundations.
Who is missing among the rubble?

Downed trees and power lines,
debris scattered for miles,
infrastructure crippled.
What is salvageable?

Uncontrollable tears, lives devastated.
They clutched each other, mumbled prayers.
Clouds parted,
sunlight streamed hope.

Adrift

We lie upon a woolen blanket
spread on the chilled ground
and gaze at the autumn night sky.
An imaginary harpist
strums hypnotic melodies
on Lyra's strings.

Our minds, ships laden with worldly cargo,
sail through the cobalt sea illuminated by stars.
The sky is alive with splashes from
Pices, the fish, and Delphinus, the dolphin.

We cast our nets with hopes
of capturing thc illusory beauty,
adrift in the night sky, our destination unknown.
Stargazers, we seek welcomed ports.

Short Poems

Penned Dear John letter
Deposited in mailbox
Irretrievable
Emotions fluctuated
Moved forward with no regrets

Forsaken lovers
Reminders scratch at hearts
Hope scars will heal
Forget the past, move on
Begin with a glance then smile

Swinging their clasped hands
A romantic moonlight stroll
Their new beginning
Ocean waves wash away
Memories of past lovers

Winding road lined with memories
Risks involved in retrieving
Some better left behind

Grandmother's treasure
Cream, peach cameo locket
Laid in a pawn shop window
Succumbed to financial need

Sole Mate

Frayed strap, broken heel, scuffed leather
worn beyond repair.
Replicating life.
Slumped in her chair,
enveloped by her robe,
clinging to memories.
One more dance.

Unacknowledged Truth

Like many of her sisters,
she works her first shift job.
Her monthly salary barely
covers her bills. Weary,
stressed, she begins
her "second shift" at 5 p.m.

She prepares another dinner
of mac'n cheese, monitors homework,
does necessary laundry,
limited clothing, but clean.
She attends soccer games,
PTA meetings, church.

After evening baths,
her children plea,
"Let us stay up longer."
"Ten minutes, no more."
A bedtime story,
forehead kisses.

She tiptoes down the hallway.
Old, wooden boards creak
like her achy joints.
She places her hands
on her lower back.
Her kitchen chores await.

She sits, elbows on table,
chin rests in her sticky hands
from making peanut butter
and jelly sandwiches for lunch.
She squints at the calendar,
shakes her head.

She shuffles
to her bedroom,
kicks off her shoes,
collapses on her bed.
To do lists swirl
in her head.

Cast Iron Mother

The widow slings an infant on her left hip while
older children cling to her dress, they plod
through California beet and cotton fields,
she shields eyes from setting suns.
She rubs her lower back, wraps her raw hands.

Like her, like Florence Owen Thompson,
"The Migrant Mother," you wear tattered clothes.
Dirt cakes in wrinkles; muscles and joints ache.
Twisting your hair between your fingers,
you hang your head and sigh.

A single parent, you balance trays,
scrub floors, restock shelves. You clutch
the steering wheel of your safe haven
as you gape at appliance cardboard dwellings
under Atlanta's Jackson Street Bridge.

You stand with swollen feet in long
unemployment and soup kitchen lines
with your children, your baby birds,
crying to be fed, tugging at your jeans.
You bend down, stroke their heads, hushhh.

Altered Silhouette

The evening light casts my silhouette upon a clean canvas. Flesh stretches over my skeletal frame. The left side lies flatter now. My long awaited desire for smaller breasts arrived, in part, a month ago. I had dreamed of cosmetic breast reduction. Cancer and my surgeon chose a different sculpturing method. I feel lop-sided. Now my fitted clothes pucker then hang loosely on one side. My new scars and image grate as a sand granule irritates an oyster. Like a pearl, my inner beauty is not lost. For self-preservation, I learn new brush strokes: fabrics, styles, and accessories. I apply colors that enhance my natural features. As I work on my impressionistic self-portrait, I am healing.

Yet, We Laughed

Left breast, cancer removed
Cleaner margins needed
No plastic surgery
Done with scalpels and sutures
Not ready to laugh.

Drove home from the hospital
Stopped for frozen yogurt
My young daughter remarked,
"You've been discabooberated."
Laughter filled our car.

Later blocked for radiation
Purplish-black periods
Dotted my chest, perhaps a
Game of connect the dots
Laughter filled the medical room.

Twenty years later only
Scars and tattooed dots remain
My oncologist remarked,
"You're quite asymmetrical."
"But I can maintain my balance."
Laughter filled the exam room.

Radiated left breast firm
Droopy, larger right breast
Gravity took its toll
Disguised under my clothes
Content, still cancer-free,
Reaping laughter's healing.

Danger Below

sweet cornbread baked in the oven
the tattered screen door of the farmhouse
propped open with a broom handle
she stood in the kitchen doorway

beads of sweat trickled down her back
flies buzzed around her matted hair
she fanned herself with last week's newspaper

she struggled in the rural abyss
her steel blue eyes stared at wilted corn stalks
her demeanor was cold like an iceberg

she guarded her thoughts, massive ice chunks
drifted in the North Atlantic
her feelings hidden beneath the
surface of her exposed, parched skin

I never got to know her, refusing
to submerge and explore her iced layers
fearful of uncovering hidden secrets
frozen within her unsettled mind

Enlightened Silence

Oppressive thoughts hide in the recesses of my mind
Like lurking shadows, memories, in a desolate alley.
I am intimidated by the darkness, crippled by the stench.

Shhh, listen to the silence.
It will not betray you.
Listen to love and hope.
Reflect and empower yourself.

Refuse to be a victim held captive,
Choked by self-doubt,
Stifled by societal constraints,
Battered by abuse.

Through silence gain wisdom.
Break your chains of dependence,
Memories that render you helpless.

Silence your naysayers.
Affirm your self-worth.
Pass through the darkness
Into the light, follow your dreams.

Harmonious Healer

Turquoise connects sky blues to aquamarine seas,
life giving elements of air and water.
As my self-confidence ebbs and flows,
I seek seclusion on a tropical island
surrounded by soothing, tepid, blue-green waters.
Rainbow and tetra fish shimmer
peacefully beneath the surface.
Rhythmic waves lap, spiritual lullabies,
attempt to calm my inner turmoil.

My thoughts churn like ocean surf
until wisdom glows, resembles
dazzling, bioluminescence swirls.
I taste, smell salty spray,
transport myself to pristine Alaskan waters.
Stunning, turquoise tinted, glacial ice
awakens my emotions as
ice calves into northern waters.
My worries break off, drift away,
melt in warmer seas.

Turquoise, a master healer,
adorns my physical being
while it purifies my mind,
realigns my energy,
restores my inner harmony.

Discarded

Curiosity brings us,
best friends, down a gravel road
beyond the Crawford family cemetery.
We walk the wooden, planked foot bridge
across meandering Tabs Creek.

Stop, cock our heads, faces skyward,
gaze at the scarred maple tree branches,
laden with hundreds of shoes,
exposed on leafless limbs.

Why discard footwear here?
    youthful secrecy,
    adolescent whim,
    in memoriam

An anonymous,
random work of art—
    red high-topped sneakers
    olive green tactical boots
    royal blue tennis shoes
    ivory toddler shoes
dangle undisturbed.

Colorful, collage of footwear relics—
    alternate trophy for a victory
        or reminder of a loss,
    remembrance of first
        or strategic steps
attracted onlookers before us.

Tempted to toss our laced shoes
high into the tree as a
token of our friendship
till disappointment strikes us.

Battered by winds,
perhaps struck by lightning,
broken branches succumbed
to the weight of sun-faded,
weather-tattered shoes
like lives worn by time.

We choose not to fling our shoes,
hopeful for more shared experiences,
unlike these forgotten soles,
which foliage will hide again.

Transformation

Larva mimics bird droppings
gray streaked, creamy lumps
pupa readies for permutation

chrysalis tears, reveals
iridescent blue bands of
Red-spotted Purple Admiral

flutters within mixed woodlands
seeks nourishment from
tree sap, fermented fruit, mud puddles

Person mimics most popular
employs social media savvy
laughs, cries, guarded within

one's social circle
seeks acceptance, tests parameters
longs for self-identity

hormonal changes, adjustments
with hope of emerging a
reliant, beautiful butterfly

Silent Stroll

Selected river stones
    purposely placed
Tranquil pilgrimage
    following concentric circles
Worldly thoughts silenced
    by heart beats, breaths
Relinquished control
    immersed in stillness
Torn between losing oneself
    and finding oneself

Once reached center
    pausing to reflect
Listening to inner feelings
    seeking clarity
Life lessons resonate
    as one resumes the pathway
Leaving better grounded
    than when I entered

Essence Renewed

Dusk to dawn light blinks off.
Sun peeks over horizon.
Subtle, pastel clouds
streak across brightening sky.

Songbirds awaken,
nudge me to get my first
cup of dark roasted coffee.
Aroma complements earthy scents.

Dew sparkles like diamonds.
I tiptoe across the grass to
my wrought-iron chair.
Sit, sip, observe, listen.

Mourning doves coo
perched on a wire.
Peaceful moment to reflect and
give thanks for country solitude.

Nature presents her gifts,
enriches my spirit,
rejuvenates me
for another day.

Solitary Walk

After the trees clothe themselves
in emerald foliage, their branches
extend me an invitation.

Tree oils and damp earthiness infuse.
Forest air offers reprieve from pollution.
Tree-lined path provides tranquility.

Wonderment of woods embraces my being,
releases me from worldly demands.
I discover apricot lichen
adheres to hickory shagbark.
Spongy reindeer moss

cushions the forest floor.
Umbrella toadstools huddle,
periwinkle florets decorate the ground,
aromatic sassafras awakens,
fuchsia rosebud delights.

Carolina cherry laurel blossoms
appear cloud-like, daffodils and
forsythias elicit sunshine, purple goblet
tulip magnolia blooms catch raindrops.

Eastern box turtle crawls from underbrush,
five-lined skink basks in filtered sunlight on rotting log,
marbled salamander scurries to capture earthworm.

My contemplative immersion like the
revival of resurrection fern fronds.

Remembrance

Ruby-throated hummingbirds,
Red Admiral butterflies
await warm nectar within
funnel-shaped yellow, orange,
pink gladioli blossoms.

My grandmother's etched glass vase
sits on the dining room table,
awaits her favorite early summer
'Black Star' gladioli with
velvety, maroon blooms
cradled by sword-shaped leaves.

Towering spires with multiple,
colorful blossoms will grace
my flower garden and
complement my grandmother's vase.
Show stopping, spectacular blooms
will eclipse the delicate fragrance.

I sit at the oak table,
sip a cup of hot tea,
picture a freshly cut bouquet.
Short-lived beauties, like Grandma,
remain etched in my memory.

Worm-Ridden Republic

Over two hundred years ago, our ancestors attempted to ensure our nation's sovereignty, indirect democracy, and civil liberties with the ratification of the *U.S. Constitution* and the *Bill of Rights*. Yet, today there are those who challenge the validity of the documents for our contemporary society. Some argue that the *Constitution* paralyzes governmental operations. An imbalance of power among the three branches of government exists. The burdensome amendment process delays change. Is our government held hostage to such critics? Are our rights stripped away in the name of homeland security or social welfare?

This nation, a cradle, has endured bumpy rocking by politicians, lobbyists, and special interest groups. Now the wood appears worn and worm-ridden. It slowly rots and disintegrates before our eyes. Awaken the sleeping baby, our nation's apathetic citizens, swaddled in the cradle, a government "of the people, by the people, for the people" in need of repair before it is no longer salvageable.

River Gifts

In my daredevil youth, on steamy summer afternoons,
seeking the thrill of rafting down a rushing river,
jostled by the rapids,
dodging logs,
ricocheting off rocks,
bobbing up and down like a cork,
listening to the water grumble,
beseeching me, "Slow down."
Intensely focusing on my course,
scraping past more nested boulders,
taking risks, and overcoming challenges.
Exhilarating feats despite the cost—
If only I had sought an eddy
for respite and reflection.

Now in my advanced years,
preferring more tranquil rides,
tube floating down a calm river,
spying my reflection in the glassy surface,
dangling my feet and hands in the refreshing water,
drifting down the placid channel,
cradled by the gentle current,
welcoming the river's gurgles,
"Take it easy; enjoy the scenery."

Appreciating the shallow, amber water
transitioning to deep, bottle green at mid-stream,
sunlight shimmering off the riverbed's sediment,
fish gently tickling my toes,
a wood duck paddling gracefully,
turtles sunning on a fallen tree trunk,
birds cheerfully serenading,
and honeysuckle's sweet, floral fragrance
wafting in the breeze.

A predictable course with no unforeseen obstacles,
just cruising through life,
confident that I'm prepared
for whatever lies ahead.

Having traveled down this meandering river many times,
I now bid the river a final good-bye.
Soon, too, will I be retiring,
peaceful and content.

Aged

Dusty, moldy, musty
Yellowed, brown stained
Wrinkled, tattered pages
Faded ink, missing leaves
Broken spine
Forgotten on the shelf
Few visitors

Antiseptic smell
Darkened, liver spots
Wrinkled, translucent skin
Gray, thinning hair
Achy back, swollen joints
Forgotten in the home
Few visitors

Have all their pages been written?

Priceless, rare editions
Stores of wisdom
Treasured stories

Will all their pages be read?

Scarred Resilience

she rubs her fingertips
over fresh and faded scars
that serve as emblems of courage
badges of her survival

some painful reminders
others joyful memories
these scars represent
her capacity for life

when she wakens to stormy days
she refuses to succumb
to the squalls, with fortitude
and sense of purpose

she scrutinizes the river
drowns her fears, alters her course
adapts and maneuvers rapids
chooses to embrace change

rebounds from adversity
thankful for smoother waters
time to nurture herself

with an optimistic outlook
she acknowledges her scars
as a lifetime earned

Virgo's Light

Virgo, last goddess to live among the ancient Greeks,
saw their goodness, shared their prosperity until

Dark clouds of greed, corruption encompassed the earth,
overshadowed the virtuous.

Distraught, Virgo spread her angelic wings,
soared into the night sky, took her place among the stars.

Each spring we scan the southern sky for Virgo's constellation
low on the horizon between Leo and Libra.

We search for the bright light of Spica held in her left hand,
a semblance of Lady Liberty's torch. Perhaps to guide and

enlighten us, so we may find resolution
before we, too, rest in the heavens.

Waning Time

Fine grains of white sand
flow silently from
one hourglass
globe to the other.

Each grain,
an increment of time,
a new beginning, an end,
a life, a death.

Marks the passage of time
without interruption,
the inevitability
of a life cycle.

One globe empties, void of life,
as one fills with grains
of sand, a mound of
life experiences.

About the Author

Suzanne Cottrell, an outdoor enthusiast and retired teacher, lives with her husband and a rescued dog in rural Piedmont North Carolina. She enjoys reading, writing, knitting, hiking, Pilates, Tai Chi, and yoga. Her poetry has appeared in numerous online and print anthologies and journals including the *Best Emerging Poets Series, The Avocet, Plum Tree Tavern, The Pangolin Review, Poetry Quarterly,* and *Burningword Literary Journal.* She was the recipient of the 2017 Rebecca Lard Poetry Award, *Poetry Quarterly,* Prolific Press. She is the author of two poetry chapbooks: *Gifts of the Seasons, Autumn and Winter* and *Gifts of the Seasons, Spring and Summer,* published by Kelsay Books.

https://suzanneswords.com

www.ingramcontent.com/pod-product-compliance
Lightning Source LLC
Chambersburg PA
CBHW021027090426
42738CB00007B/934